English Language Teachers as Program Administrators

Dan J. Tannacito

English
Language
Teacher
Development
Series

Thomas S. C. Farrell,
Series Editor

tesol
international
association

Typeset in Janson and Frutiger
by Capitol Communications, LLC, Crofton, Maryland USA
and printed by Gasch Printing, LLC, Odenton, Maryland USA

TESOL International Association
1925 Ballenger Avenue
Alexandria, Virginia 22314 USA
Tel 703-836-0774 • Fax 703-836-7864

Publishing Manager: Carol Edwards
Cover Design: Tomiko Breland
Copyeditor: Suzi Hersey

TESOL Book Publications Committee
John I. Liontas, Chair

Maureen S. Andrade	Joe McVeigh
Jennifer Lebedev	Gail Schafers
Robyn L. Brinks Lockwood	Lynn Zimmerman

Project overview: John I. Liontas and Robyn L. Brinks Lockwood
Reviewer: Soonyoung Hwang An

ISBN 9781931185042

Contents

About the Author

Dan J. Tannacito is Emeritus Professor of TESOL/Applied Linguistics. He previously directed an intensive English program for 35 years and was former director of the doctoral and master's degree programs in the United States and Turkey.

Dedication

To Mon, sparse words on a pale page to say thank you.

Series Editor's Preface

The English Language Teacher Development (ELTD) Series consists of a set of short resource books for English language teachers that are written in a jargon-free and accessible manner for all types of teachers of English (native and nonnative speakers of English, experienced and novice teachers). The ELTD Series is designed to offer teachers a theory-to-practice approach to English language teaching, and each book offers a wide variety of practical teaching approaches and methods for the topic at hand. Each book also offers opportunities for teachers to interact with the materials presented. The books can be used in preservice settings or in-service courses and by individuals looking for ways to refresh their practice.

Dan Tannacito's book *English Language Teachers as Program Administrators* explores different approaches to administering a language program and the various challenges this may present to a language teacher. Tannacito provides a comprehensive overview of how to administer a language program in an easy-to-follow guide that language teachers will find very practical for their own contexts. Topics include the benefits of becoming an English language program administrator, how to manage people in such a program, and how to design a curriculum that includes student placement in such programs. *English Language Teachers as Program Administrators* is a valuable addition to the literature in our profession.

I am very grateful to the authors who contributed to the ELTD Series for sharing their knowledge and expertise with other TESOL professionals because they have done so willingly and without any compensation to make these short books affordable to language teachers throughout the world. It was truly an honor for me to work with each of these authors as they selflessly gave up their valuable time for the advancement of TESOL.

Thomas S. C. Farrell

1

What, Me? An Administrator?

Most current English language program administrators (ELPAs) received degrees in applied linguistics or TESOL and learned the administrative side through experience and self-study. No degrees are yet offered specifically in language program management, but certificates or diplomas may be earned at the School for International Training and the Monterey Institute of International Studies in the United States. Despite the fact that, for many years, courses in program administration have been proposed as essential to teacher development, only a few MA/MEd or PhD programs in North America offer them (University of Arizona, University of Utah, and Georgia State University are exceptions).

Because many English language teachers, both practicing and in preparation, may have the interest and skills to succeed in English language program administration, the approach taken in this book is to introduce this field through the concept of self-directed development. Whatever your level of experience with English language programs, the time is now to begin your preparation for a career as an ELPA. Enrollment of international and other ESL students in colleges and universities in North America is expected to continue to grow (IIE, 2011), creating a continuing need for administrators to manage these larger student bodies.

This book focuses on the administration of a single type of English language program, representative of more than 1,000 domestic sites and many international ones. These intensive English programs (IEPs) are self-supporting English language courses or programs offered for a variety of purposes (vocational, academic, etc.) primarily for international students preparing to attend colleges and universities at the undergraduate and graduate levels. English as a second language (ESL) is the main subject taught in these programs, usually on a full-time and intensive basis (see Homeland Security for U.S. requirements) in anglophone countries, and at large universities internationally where English is the medium of instruction in degree programs.

Participation may be mandatory or voluntary, depending on the admission status to the receiving university. Ownership of IEPs may be public (i.e., state-owned) or commercial. Students attend IEPs for a variety of reasons, the most common being (a) to enhance their language skills for personal growth and development; (b) to prepare themselves for studies at U.S. high schools, colleges, universities, or other educational programs; (c) to augment their linguistic and cultural knowledge as exchange students for a limited period of time abroad; and (d) to acquire language/content-specific training (English for specific purposes) on a short-term basis.

Benefits of Becoming an ELPA

The culture of administration, in certain ways, can be far different from that of the classroom. For most teachers, it calls for new ways of communicating with others and of negotiating institutional politics. But many of the responsibilities of ELPAs are based on the content of English language teaching or extensions of teaching skills: planning, executing, evaluating. Still, many responsibilities go beyond teaching into management, policy making, marketing, negotiating, finance, and counseling, among other domains (White, Hockley, van der Horst Jansen, & Laughner, 2008; Christison & Stoller, 1997, 2012). Developing the breadth of knowledge and synthesis of skills and experience required to be a successful ELPA—in a word, personal growth—is perhaps the foremost benefit of a career in this area.

First, English language teachers often want to make a difference. Changing lives is at the heart of why teachers become teachers. Going beyond the walls of the classroom to effect the changes that improve policy, practice, and pedagogy is vital to accomplishing change. Second, conclusions about teaching and learning drawn from management theory often differ radically from ideas and viewpoints that emerge from the practice of teaching and research in applied linguistics. Grounded in the classroom and teacher collaboration, English language teachers offer a distinct perspective on curricular planning, supervision, and policy making enacted in administrative roles. Third, the administration of English language programs is literally at the crossroads of cultures in a postsecondary environment which many teachers-becoming-administrators enjoy tremendously. Finally, too few teachers may immediately recognize the collaborative research opportunities afforded by an administrative position. Provided that research does not interfere with teaching and adheres strictly to ethical practices, it can greatly benefit the IEP.

Hence, taking on administrative functions, either part time or full time, should not be regarded as a burdensome distraction but as a valuable asset. Becoming an ELPA enables a teacher to promote cultural understanding, effect educational change, and grow personally and professionally.

Supplementing Formal Education

Because there is no single path to successful preparation as an ELPA, you may start with one or more degrees in diverse disciplines ranging from higher education to applied linguistics. Whatever your core education, you will need to supplement it with additional courses or training because this is an interdisciplinary area of study. For a teacher with a TESOL degree, the most frequently mentioned areas where coursework would be a benefit are organizational theory, budgeting, ethics, program design, marketing/promotion, immigration, human resources, employment, technology, immigration law, testing and assessment, leadership, higher education, curriculum development, personnel management, classroom observation, teacher supervision, interviewing, materials and purchasing management, social networking, grant writing, database management, intercultural training, and descriptive and predictive research methodologies. This list may seem long, so it is advisable to spread out this supplementary formal training over time.

Determining your mix of desirable supplementary courses encourages further growth and overcoming constraints that every student inevitably encounters (e.g., how many electives from each department can a graduate student take?). Here is a list of strategies to build the supplement:

(a) Search the course catalog for relevant courses available in departments other than your own. Talk to the instructor about your interest.

(b) Explore credit options within your degree and the resources available.

(c) Do an internship in a division of the university which deals with an area of relevance.

(d) Enroll in relevant courses under nondegree status at nearby institutions or online.

(e) Attend relevant workshops offered regularly by professional associations and commercial vendors.

(f) Design a research project under an existing course that focuses on topics within ELPA.

(g) Volunteer to work in a specific role (e.g., tutor) in order to observe or shadow an administrator.

Roles of ELPAs

An administrator, broadly conceived, can be considered to be a person who has authority to lead and manage people, practices, materials, and policies in an educational unit. There are a wide variety of administrative roles which a teacher can take on—in part or in whole—within a language program environment. Every language program has a somewhat different configuration of roles, depending on its history, size, resources, mission, and so forth. Each of these roles requires some skills unique to the position, and each involves functions of varying complexity. Most programs advertise job descriptions which detail the required functions and the essential skills. The following list gives one perspective on role positions:

Activities Coordinator—International students want opportunities to visit places and meet people with whom they can use the language they are learning in a new country. Part travel agent, part cultural interpreter, this role allows much one-to-one interaction with students from a variety of cultures and relies on your local knowledge of American culture.

Assistant Director—This person usually serves in the absence of the director and, depending on the size and complexity of the IEP unit, may be responsible for one or more positions focused on finance, personnel, policy, teaching, record management, immigration, student performance and behavior, and so forth.

Curriculum Coordinator—Designs, organizes, coordinates, and evaluates courses at multiple levels of proficiency and instruction to fit the mission and the learning goals of the IEP. The coordinator must know what is effective in teaching students from various cultures and the state of the art in all matters of curriculum, including testing and evaluation at times as well.

Director—The leading figure in the IEP unit directly responsible to a higher administrator, whether department chair, dean, or vice-president in a university setting. The director must have a detailed knowledge of all internal aspects of the unit and must represent the unit in relation to the broader campus and community constituencies.

The director may have status as a faculty member, an administrator, or a combination of both, depending on specific institutions.

Marketing Specialist—When an IEP must recruit and balance its student population and maintain enrollment levels, often a specialist is needed who knows the principles and tools of marketing and understands English language education markets.

Records Manager—helps students enroll or change courses, enter the university computing system, check and pay bills, and seek financial assistance. Accurately records everything from student background information, prior education, test scores, placement information, and grades. Very important to this position are an orientation toward orderliness, accuracy, and detail as well as facility with databases and recognition of privacy and security of student information.

Student Advisor—This problem-focused position requires good local knowledge and a mature perception of what makes for a safe and enjoyable sojourn for students, whether focused on academic goals or on the inevitable contact issues of living in a new place with people one hardly knows and unfamiliar legal and cultural norms.

Teacher Trainer/Supervisor—The experienced classroom teacher can serve as a trainer or supervisor of other teachers in order to maintain uniformly high standards of instruction or to introduce new curriculum or new teachers to an existing curriculum. Often supervisors have the additional role of evaluating teachers on a periodic basis and providing feedback for their improvement. Thus, interpersonal as well as trained observation skills are essential.

Testing Coordinator—IEPs need to determine new students' academic level, required courses, promotional guidelines, and graduation requirements. For this role the ELPA must know standardized as well as alternative testing procedures, how to train others in a coordinated effort when large numbers of students are involved, and accurate and secure record keeping procedures.

Technology Coordinator—Main role is to infuse technology into curriculum through the use of multiple media, Internet, and distance tools. May also work with curriculum coordinator to lead the professional development of teachers in the IEP environment as well as handle the direct training of students.

Tutor Trainer/Supervisor—Near-peer tutoring has been applied widely and effectively in university settings. For this role, ELPAs need an intuitive sense of the language as opposed to knowing "why" grammar is the way it is, for example. Although training varies by IEP site, it can include dealing with issues of cross-cultural interaction, materials appropriate in level and content, and other developmental issues when assisting ESL students to become more autonomous with the language. A proportionate use of nonnative-English-speaking tutors is an advantage.

REFLECTIVE BREAK

- Brainstorm a list of the top three ELPA roles that are most relevant to your current situation.

- Prioritize your list and think about why you have chosen each role.

Teacher Self-Directed Development

Professional development is a process of continuous growth (Richards & Farrell, 2005). This statement applies to managing language learning education as well as to teaching. Self-directed development means the willingness to manage one's self in the pursuit of this growth and to control one's learning toward personal goals. A teacher's development of administrative competence may begin during formal education, as discussed above, but will continue through self-directed development afforded by opportunities and experiences. Use the *wedge technique* in career development: enter where you have strength and learn lateral positions before moving up.

Activities

One strategy that can help you self-direct your development as an ELPA is to seek out activities that have an administrative element, such as the following:

Apprenticeship or Internship—There may be no better way to understand the knowledge and skills required of an administrative position than to serve an apprenticeship or internship under a director, assistant director, or curriculum specialist.

Volunteer at Existing Sites—Spend time volunteering with a variety of offices or organizations involved with ESL students. For example, serve as a librarian in the teachers' resource library in order to become familiar with resources, or volunteer to take students on an outing to a site you are familiar with in order to reinforce the skills they are currently learning.

On-the-Job Training—Seek out opportunities to gain some training officially or as an auditor in workshops and other venues as they become available. Sit in on methodology or technology demonstrations where permitted.

Offer Free Tutoring—Post a notice at the library or where ESL students congregate, indicating your availability to assist an ESL student with a specific task, such as editing a paper. Or volunteer at the IEP or to assist a teacher you like to develop your listening skills.

Join Special Interest Sections—Meeting with program administrator groups and joining the conversation lets you learn about practitioners' concerns.

Tools

In addition to the activities above, some of the following tools for self-development will help you to evolve as an administrator.

Shadowing—Ask one or two administrative personnel to allow you (at their convenience) to shadow them for a day or two to learn what they do and how they do it. Shadowing is an unobtrusive way to closely observe.

Interviewing—Create a list of questions about a position, focused on a particular area (e.g., budgeting); email a couple of people in the same administrative position but in two locations and interview both via email. Compare their responses.

Observing—If an ELPA visits a classroom, ask to accompany unobtrusively or during individual student sessions in an advisor's office.

Journaling—After you shadow, interview, and observe an ELPA, write descriptions as well as impressions as soon as possible afterwards. Make sure to create questions in your journal so you can follow up.

Teaming/Friendships—Team up with an administrator or teacher to discuss their work experience informally over coffee or a beer.

REFLECTIVE BREAK

- Review the lists of Activities and Tools above and choose which tools are best suited to accomplishing the activities.

2

Managing People in English Language Programs

Most of the revenue in an IEP is generated from student enrollment, whereas the bulk of expenses are usually devoted to staff and teachers. From the top of the chain of authority in an English language program on down, one thing remains the same: IEPs cannot flourish without successful student recruitment. Developing the knowledge and skills in this area will enhance your value as an ELPA. In addition, the alliance between administrators and teachers strengthens the intensive English program itself. Thus student recruitment and forging alliances are probably the two wisest avenues to develop as a teacher-becoming-administrator.

Student Recruitment

It all begins with students—and ends there, too. Depending on your role, you may want to assess your current student enrollment situation. Since changes in enrollment patterns can happen abruptly in IEPs, it is usually necessary to collect data from at least 3 years back to understand the current situation.

REFLECTIVE BREAK

- What data do you think you need to collect to create an effective recruitment plan?

In addition to your institutional data, you will need access to information about which countries or areas are sending significant numbers of students to North America (see IIE, 2011). Data on attendance dates can give a fairly good indication about when different countries or areas are able to attend. You can determine the different semester start dates designated for student-exchange semesters, as well as various graduation dates around the world. Institutional data on addresses and contacts is also important if you wish to maintain or re-establish connections with the former sources of IEP student recruitment. Some of this data may already be compiled by departments such as an Office of International Affairs.

To effectively monitor or change the enrollment patterns in an IEP, you need to become aware of pre-existing agreements with individual universities and those international exchange consortiums with whom your larger entity may have membership. If you are directing a program—or are delegated enrollment responsibility—you need to know who has authority to create agreements and what the terms may be. Undoubtedly, this involves working with other administrators outside and above your position. But it may be among the fastest ways to increase enrollments if you have prior contacts with universities and organizations which you wish to introduce to your context. Assessing your current situation with respect to patterns of current enrollment and pre-existing agreements positions you to create a plan for change.

Changing Recruitment

What do you need to change, if anything, about your student enrollment? Of course, this may not be your sole decision, and it certainly is well-advised to consult other administrators who also have responsibility to plan international recruitment.

REFLECTIVE BREAK

- Is there a need to increase student enrollment at your IEP? At what level and to what extent?

- Is there a desire—even a policy goal—to have better country/region distribution among your international students? What regions need to be better represented in your IEP?

In a multi-proficiency program where curriculum is organized by levels, consider if it may be effective to have more students in lower levels, for example. Does the unit have an uneven number of new students at different times of the year, pointing to a semester (e.g., summer) when increases could be targeted? Most important is to avoid the phenomenon of successfully high enrollments in one year but disastrously low enrollments in the next. These changes require careful and long-range plans because enrollment of admitted students is from 6 months to 1 year out.

In creating a recruitment plan, begin with goals and limits, whether you are working with a newly developed program or a relatively established one. The number of international students in a particular English language program may be governed by mission statements pertaining to the creation of a multicultural campus environment (e.g., 5–20% of the student body). Also consider the constraints for recruitment dictated by the program itself. Is there space allocated or available to accommodate additional students in classrooms and housing? To what extent does the unit have the human resources—in particular, the available trained teaching staff—to offer the curriculum to more students? For instance, do you have teachers knowledgeable about the needs of true beginners? Do you wish to manage enrollment so as to increase class/level size but limit it to instructionally effective levels? If so, you may want to increase the overall number of students at intermittent times of the year, at various levels within the program, and from different countries or regions within the limits of the physical and human resources available.

REFLECTIVE BREAK

- Which question above resonates most in your current situation?

Spot Recruitment

As mentioned, student recruitment takes time, but there are some short-term actions, or *spot recruitment*, that can add significantly to a plan:

- Existing unmet language learning needs of the currently enrolled international student population (e.g., spouse classes that can be created)

- For unmet needs, offer workshops, individual courses, very short term training opportunities

- Tap into those with language learning needs in unserved communities outside the location of your English language program (e.g., advertise in native language newspapers in the community)

- Collaborate on joint programs that are mutually beneficial, such as other English language programs in the community serving immigrant groups or those in a network of universities

- Provide short-term instruction (e.g., summer or during breaks) that prepare students admitted to other colleges or universities nearby who may not have their own language programs

- Collaborate with domestic or international partners (see Dimmitt & Dantas-Whitney, 2002)

The following considerations are part of long-range planning for spot recruiting:

- Offer a fuller range of programs to potential students

- Expand your English language program if it provides only language learning for academically bound students

- Existing university certificate programs—short-term, nondegree business executive programs or health professional programs— may be willing to enroll international visitors concurrently or subsequently to an English for specific purposes program

- Design a grant-based short-term program in response to state, national, or international granting opportunities. Of course, grants are competitive, but the more experience you gain, the better your chances of adding spot recruitment to an emerging recruitment plan.

Finally, use your own resourcefulness in making contacts. There is nothing more important than word of mouth, which makes it vital to provide a quality educational experience to the students attending the language program. Other easy sources of contacts are alumni from the language program, international student organizations on campus, faculty who have vested interest in a country or region for personal (e.g., origin/marriage) or academic (e.g., Fulbright scholarships) reasons, embassies and consulates, and departments on campus—especially graduate programs—interested in providing provisional or conditional admission to students from certain countries.

REFLECTIVE BREAK

- What populations mentioned above are possible communities for spot recruitment in your context?

- Who would you contact to initiate an inquiry about language needs?

Having a presence at professional associations and conferences helps build contacts in the network of international educators. Some to consider are TESOL International Association's Program Administration Interest Section (PAIS), National Association of International Educators (NAFSA), Association for Supervisors and Curriculum Development (ASCD), and the International Society for Technology in Education (ISTE).

It may not be economical to employ individuals or companies who recruit international students, but some recruiters charge their fees directly to students recruited. This procedure avoids any potential legal conflict where private corporations are not permitted to recruit students at a public university. Every language program should have instruments for recruitment such as a fully developed website, dedicated advertising outlets, and direct mail lists (see Heaney, 2009, for additional ideas).

A good recruitment plan requires some expenses, and it will be necessary to budget for travel, technology support, print advertising, and hosting of lunches for faculty and alumni. Economic and political climates influence, at the macro level, timing of international student flows into intensive English programs. For example, countries announce new scholarship programs for study abroad (e.g., Saudi

Arabia in the early 2000's), countries with significant international student presence in the United States may suddenly cut off or suspend the outflow of students (e.g., Iran in the late 1970's), or countries change internal language policy, affecting the need for English abroad (e.g., Malaysia). The availability of federal grants is often driven by macro politics. Moreover, a weak dollar abroad usually promotes the rise of international student applications. Hence, effective language program management depends on recruitment that takes into consideration multiple dimensions at both the micro and the macro levels.

Managing students in an English language program goes beyond recruiting and involves student admission, orientation, advising, and policy making. Many resources are available that cover these highly important areas in maintaining a quality program (see Pennington, 1991; White et al., 2008; Christison & Murray, 2009).

Selecting Instructional Personnel

ELPAs can have either sole responsibility or a subsidiary role in selecting instructional personnel. Important factors in the hiring process are presented in the following sections.

Mission

Hiring instructors is directly related to mission. Every language program needs a clear and detailed mission statement that is regularly revised and that fits with the stated missions of its larger institutional context. An IEP mission that includes providing multicultural education to its students, including international students who may be attending the intensive English program, must focus on ways to carry that mission forward. If such provisions are not part of the mission, then developing this concept may be an important clarifying step in leadership by IEP administrators.

Social Representation

When managing human resources, meeting federal standards for employment is an absolute necessity. But issues of social representation (gender, native language, race, and ethnicity) within language programs permit choices that relate to how a staff or faculty is hired and hence perceived by current and future students.

Native language is the last, yet unrecognized, civil right that impacts IEPs, especially in hiring personnel. IEPs have traditionally been biased toward employing native-English-speaking teachers due to student demand. IEP leaders have an important opportunity in creating an equitable hiring policy of native- and nonnative-English-speaking teachers.

In a similar way, international students may be negatively influenced about their perceptions of race in the United States—either exaggerating the value of whiteness or denigrating that of color, extending even to their own race. Whether the issue is native language or race, the value of socially representing multiracial and nonnative-English-speaking teachers on staff is a social benefit for students that can become an educational one, too. Sometimes students who come from fairly homogeneous linguistic, ethnic, or racial backgrounds may not realize initially that they are likely to encounter multiracial, multi-ethnic faculty at their university in North America beyond the IEP itself.

REFLECTIVE BREAK

- What would you say to students who came to you to complain that their teacher was not a native speaker, or was not white?

Status of Teachers

One of the thorniest issues facing an administrator of a language program in creating an effective and satisfied work force is the status of teachers as employees. Are they faculty or nonfaculty? Full time or part time? Graduate students or nonstudents? To what extent can undergraduates be used? These issues are usually bound up with those of accreditation, labor relations, and negotiation (see University Consortium of Intensive English Programs (UCIEP); Christison & Stoller, 2012).

Teacher Evaluation

Evaluation is one of the principal functions that must be performed by those who lead IEPs, particularly the evaluation of staff, teachers, and students. Of these, perhaps the most complicated to evaluate are teachers because in a language program the major impact of their work (i.e., student learning) is not directly observable. In many places there is a standard, historically motivated procedure in place, applying to all faculty across disciplines and involving various constituencies, usually students, peers, and supervisors. Experience within a system is needed before one can address the effectiveness and equity of processes that are in place. Where there are none established, it behooves the leadership of English language programs to apply common framework professional standards (TESOL, 2003, 2012) and to develop their own process to accomplish national and local goals. Effective ideas include assembling a design team of representatives of the groups affected by the performance of teachers—students, teachers, and institutional representatives—as well as collaborating with teachers to develop a teacher evaluation instrument.

Mentoring

IEPs need to provide teachers with the opportunity to work with mentors who are not involved in assessment of teachers. Mentors should be chosen by protégés with their consent rather than assigned. Hence, leadership in this area involves creating optimal conditions for a mentoring relationship. This also means that experienced teachers need support to serve as mentors due to the significant time commitment, which may take the form of release from duties or the provision of additional benefits such as funding for travel to professional development events. Opportunities to maintain a mentoring relationship over time are important because a protégé moves through a sequence of phases, the first two of which—initiation and cultivation (Kram, 1983)—are vital for successful socialization.

Professional Development

Planning for the professional development of teachers and staff is very important for the long-term health of a unit like an IEP. Directors and their assistants should encourage a culture in which all members of the unit seek ongoing improvement in their knowledge and skills. Fortunately, unit leaders can tap into some cost-free workshops and training sessions, ranging from the use of various databases to procedures for purchasing and using transportation pools.

A teacher-becoming-administrator is perfectly positioned to lead teacher discussion circles about reflection in teaching (see Farrell, 2007, for an excellent source). A plan should also be devised to support expenses incurred in acquiring additional off-campus development even if it needs to be limited to coordination with overall program developments (e.g., aspects of planned curricular change). In any case, it is always wise to make known and explicit those policies and procedures for professional development, including who is eligible, when, where, and to what extent.

REFLECTIVE BREAK

- On a scale of 1 to 10 (10 being the highest), rate your current knowledge and experience with each category in this chapter.

- What is the most important category for you to develop to become an administrator?

3

Curriculum and Technology

The director of an IEP has institutional responsibility for the curriculum of a language program, and depending on particular institutional organizations, may delegate some academic responsibility for its development to an assistant director or curriculum coordinator. A typical and widely adopted model of design and development based on curriculum models since the 1970s includes needs analysis, goal setting, materials development, testing, teaching, and evaluation (see Brown, 1995). The approach to curricular innovation may be managed in principle (Markee, 1997) or it may be guided by well-known educational frameworks, such as Bloom's taxonomy of objectives, Gardner's eight intelligences, content-based instruction (Dimmit & Dantas-Whitney, 2002), and others.

For a novice administrator, the particular model employed at an IEP is the most practical starting point to understand the considerable detail which teachers are required to follow. Moreover, because curriculum is academic in nature, continuous change is inevitable as new ideas enter and are tested in applied linguistics and TESOL. Quoting Stoller (1992), "Innovation, the result of deliberate change, is a fundamental component of productive and progressive IEPs" (p. 1). Nonetheless, there are basic assumptions and implications underlying the curriculum of most IEPs which novice administrators need to balance along with the desire for change and innovation.

Two Assumptions

The curriculum of most IEPs usually rests on two long-standing assumptions: intensivity and multiple levels.

Intensivity

Language learning takes time, both concentrated and long term. The concept of intensivity as it applies to language programs is customarily formulated temporally—in hours of instruction per week—because classroom contact hours are a measure of exposure to the content of instruction (see UCIEP for accreditation requirements). Unlike the standard 3-hour per week foreign language class most U.S. undergraduates experience, intensive English is usually a minimum of 18 hours per week of instruction and practice, a concentration endorsed by professional and accrediting organizations. This amount of attention on a content area such as English is similar to an undergraduate's weekly course-hour load during a semester. By adopting the intensivity assumption, an IEP curriculum developer is faced with the question—what are the six or more courses (i.e., 18+ credit hours) at any given level whose aims, teaching, and materials taken together lead to accurate and speedy language learning? This distinctive design feature then leads directly to curricular challenges as well as to opportunities.

REFLECTIVE BREAK

- In your experience, what are some of the curriculum challenges for teachers and students in an intensive language program?

Multiple Levels of Instruction

The notion of multiple levels of instruction implements the idea that in the course of learning a new language, there can be multiple entry points reflecting each learner's development and proficiency. At one end of the spectrum are beginner or elementary-level learners, who attend IEPs with no prior understanding of English—except perhaps exposure to language infused by the media and other outlets throughout the world. At the other end of the spectrum is the advanced or professional level, which needs to meet the standards of the receiving institution. In between, most IEPs articulate three distinguishable levels which are considered developmental and intermediate. The IEP program level is generally conceived as an educational step in a progressive, integrated curriculum (like the notions of freshman, sophomore, etc.), with roughly homogeneous levels of instruction. Persons developing the curriculum need to take into consideration the following points:

(a) the range of proficiency specifications that are suited to each level (see ACTFL, 2012, for a current version of one influential scheme for describing proficiency)

(b) knowledge gained from fields like second language acquisition (Saville-Troike, 2006) about stages and sequences through which individual learners develop

(c) cultural considerations in the interaction of teachers, students, materials, and contexts

This complex process of curriculum development aims to meet student desires, aspirations, and needs in subsequent academic programs or worksites.

REFLECTIVE BREAK

A multilevel program usually promotes students from one level to another after a period of learning.

- Do you favor the practice social promotion, that is, advancing students with their cohort irrespective of language performance?

- What are the pros and cons of social promotion?

Transitions

Two important areas of concern in administering a multilevel language program are the beginning and the end. These critical junctures are the points where students move between educational systems or regimes. At the former point, students move from a home culture and society with its attendant expectations about the use of language and cultural behavior both in and out of the classroom. IEP teachers and tutors need to be aware of transition situations and their implications on the university's policy. For example, to what extent should the first language be used in second language education by the students and even the teacher? What aspects of curriculum are affected? How to integrate the new student into housing, friendships, and classroom interactions? (Cultural issues of representation which cause conflict in classrooms occur more often than is widely acknowledged at the beginning of programs.)

The learned cultural procedures for responding in the ESL classroom for students in cultural transition may be silence or resistance. For example, a student who is unwilling to volunteer an answer when called upon in class may become remarkably forthright if given a chance to first check her response with her group before answering. Until students learn that alternative cultural ways of responding are valid and expected in their new environment, they may be uncomfortable and appear as very different learners. Effective management of this cultural transition can be addressed by an administrator through the assignment of courses, intercultural training, mentoring, and other techniques. Prospective ELPAs can gain insight into student experience adapting to college and community life in the United States from Gebhard's (2010) *What Do International Students Think and Feel?*

REFLECTIVE BREAK

- From your experience as a teacher of culturally transitioning students at an IEP—or as an international student yourself— what approaches can help such students adapt?

Other aspects of transition that may be disorienting or difficult, even painful (Atkinson & Ramanathan, 1995), for the transitioning student are the different cultures that they encounter between intensive English programs and other university departments. If the university uses language test scores for placement, international students sometimes find themselves just missing the cut-off score or scoring higher than their actual proficiency and thus being misplaced. Finally, some self-aware students may elect to spend more time within the IEP in order to become more oriented to the language in use within the wider university context. ELPAs can be involved in innovative curricular solutions to this set of problems.

REFLECTIVE BREAK

- How could your IEP reformulate the curriculum at either the beginning or the end of the program in order to improve the transition for students and faculty?

Technology Development

Increasingly, technological changes enhance the quality of education and learning. Each generation of students seems to become more comfortable with technology. IEPs need to envision the future in which technology will be increasingly integrated into language instruction. Those who administer language programs have two key initiating roles within the IEP in improving the conditions for technological integration. The first is to clear the obstacles which may impede the use of technology in intensive English instruction. The second is to create and implement a plan to prepare teachers in the use of technology.

Obstacles

Language laboratories in intensive English programs may have been updated with contemporary digital multimedia capabilities, but language students perceive them as less than optimal, and teachers and researchers have been disappointed that an abundance of research and investment in the language lab "did not determine the optimal lab configuration and pedagogical program" for foreign language education (see Roby, 2004, p. 538). To implement a virtual lab using computer-centric Internet technology, the first task of an ELPA is to remove obstacles and create or convert the means needed to integrate new tools into language instruction (MacDonald, 2010).

Serious obstacles in producing technology for language instruction are an insufficient number of computers, limited access to computer classrooms for instruction, and outdated equipment that is incompatible with the technology employed in the wider environment. The latter situation leads to delays, costly replacement of equipment, and lack of skilled technical support services. Other obstacles include the lack of suitable software and materials. ELPAs can take on the task of surveying both students and teachers about their needs and desires to use specific technologies in environments of their choice, whether classrooms or library learning centers. The information can then be used to recommend how to reconfigure the technological infrastructure of a language program.

REFLECTIVE BREAK

- What obstacles have you encountered in teaching with technology in an intensive English program?

- How would you approach a solution?

Attitudes

Preservice teacher education has increasingly incorporated the use of technology to teach languages, yet graduates of master's programs continue to see the need for more pedagogical training and practice in using Internet tools to prepare lessons and improve their classroom management skills.

Administrators thus need to consider (a) the options available to teachers to infuse technology into the curriculum and (b) hands-on practice desired by in-service teachers to use technology to a greater extent in the classroom. The lack of such training is often associated with the lack of use of technology. ELPAs can determine the availability of technical and pedagogical support in the form of workshop series, teacher-led presentations, mentoring activities, and other ideas that will improve attitudes and raise expertise in a technology-infused curriculum.

Technology for instructional use and administrative computing is generally expensive; budgets must include support and training in addition to establishing a baseline of technology to be provided to each student (e.g., all classrooms equipped with computers; self-access labs open to ESL students and teachers). ELPAs can perform the next most important and least expensive step toward integrating technology into pedagogy: inventory all the technology and its support services that are available free of cost to teachers and students across the institution. This may include not only computing but also media resources such as video-editing equipment and software, web-based streaming media and blog services, and distance learning tools. In addition, it may be possible to acquire specialized databases, social media, and other communication technologies. As Whitbeck and Healey (1997) point out, "teachers need to adapt to new techniques for using technology in their classrooms because the definition of the classroom is changing" (p. 256).

REFLECTIVE BREAK

- What technology do you think should be introduced to teachers in your environment?

- Why?

Technology and Pedagogy

Many additional strategies are emerging for administrators to effect the infusion of technology into intensive English, but many new ideas need to be formulated and tried out. Hence, the approach to technology in pedagogy needs to be, in a sense, experimental. For example, partnering with a sister university outside the United States offers the possibility of incorporating tools for a distance-learning beginner-level intensive English course before students transition to the sister institution in the United States. This innovation might work well for IEPs that struggle with the teaching resources needed at this level, or it could be viewed as a pre-entry orientation in which teachers across institutions could collaborate in helping students make the study-abroad transition. ELPAs could do a study that compares pre-entry groups over time and a random beginner group not from the sister university. The ELPA thus has a research opportunity and a method to rigorously evaluate the innovation, an ideal project for a new administrator because the complexities of change are minimized and impact is controlled.

REFLECTIVE BREAK

- What technology would you use at the beginner level of ESL instruction in an IEP?

Teachers are key to transforming the IEP classroom into a digital-age learning environment, but administrators have an indispensable role. The most important resource available in the area of technology is standards for administrators, teachers, and students (ISTE, 2012; TESOL, 2011). The results from the teacher surveys and interviews, suggested above, can be used to compare to the national standards. Here are some examples related to curriculum from the ISTE standards that teachers can implement:

A. Facilitate technology-enhanced experiences that address content standards and student technology standards.

B. Use technology to support learner-centered strategies that address the diverse needs of students.

C. Apply technology to develop students' higher order skills and creativity.

In order to support these goals in improving the use of technology in language education, administrators need to

A. Identify, use, evaluate, and promote appropriate technologies to enhance and support instruction.

B. Facilitate and support collaborative technology-enriching learning environments conducive to innovation for improved learning.

C. Provide for learner-centered environments that use technology to meet the individual and diverse needs of learners.

Teachers-becoming-administrators are in the key position to lead innovation that addresses the gap in the use or nonuse of technology. Collaborating with more experienced IEP administrators to design and develop digital-age learning experiences is a necessary condition for success.

In addition to strong leadership from administrators, compensation (for travel, materials, specialized training, supplementary bonus, etc.) is required for the professional development of teachers to meet the standards. Service is a significant part of teacher evaluation and should clearly include the worth of participation in curricular innovation. The experienced administrator searches for satisfactory ways to return teacher investment.

REFLECTIVE BREAK

- How would you implement one of the standards listed above for teachers and administrators?

4

Administering Evaluations

Despite numerous criticisms of standardized English language tests (e.g., TOEFL, MELAB, TOEIC, IELTS, Cambridge) by researchers and ELL educators, their use remains widespread practice for admission to North American universities. The reason is primarily because of the security of the tests as well as the uniformity of administration across international contexts. Indeed, the IEP may be charged with an institutional responsibility to administer these tests to provide accurate information, such as meeting language requirement standards, to the larger divisions of general admissions or departments. Those divisions are generally more removed from both the practice of and research on language pedagogy and testing and thus more reliant on known standardized tests. Standardized tests may be used alone or in conjunction with more direct assessment, such as written essays or oral interviews to enter or exit an intensive English program.

REFLECTIVE BREAK

- Have you taken any or administered any standardized language tests yourself?

- What is your opinion of their value for the teacher or administrator?

The use of standardized language tests is troubled by seemingly intractable problems in defining the underlying concepts (e.g., proficiency, communicative competence). In addition, there is tremendous heterogeneity among modern languages, countries, states, and disciplines as to what are the legitimate categories and parameters of successful language use. Hence, seeking a common framework has become an undercurrent in recent testing research (e.g., ACTFL, 2012; Council of Europe, 1996). On the other hand, the use of direct measures is costly and time-consuming, as well as dependent on the availability of trained raters and interviewers.

The teacher-become-administrator needs a working understanding of standardized tests, alternative means of assessment, and emerging common frameworks because the field of language assessment is beginning to turn in a new direction. To paraphrase a Chinese proverb, novice administrators need to stand on two feet: the present and the future. Standardized tests serve a gate-keeping function for universities and many academic programs, a reality faced by international students (and other ELLs). Hence novice administrators ought to experience those tests for themselves. Moreover, they need to observe and participate, if possible, in the administration of standardized tests to understand more fully the procedures and situations students face in high-stakes testing.

ELPAs should have a foundation and ongoing education in testing and evaluation, which they can achieve by volunteering as a proctor in test administrations, through formal coursework, or guided self-reading. Many language teachers are familiar with Brown's (2004) classic *Language Assessment: Principles and Classroom Practices*, a readable and comprehensive starting point. To help guide teachers in the construction and use of testing in the classroom, see *Assessing Language Ability in the Classroom* (Cohen, 1994), and for a working methodology of writing assessment for program administrators, refer to Huot and Schendel (2002).

Program Placement

Language assessment can function for administrative purposes in several ways: assessment, placement, promotion, exemption, or certification. This section examines *placement* and offers the novice administrator a view into the complexities of people and context in testing.

Placement tests involve screening students for placement in an existing program of instruction. Multiple levels of instruction present a fundamental issue for placement. For example, too few levels usually leads to the formation of proficiency cohorts within a class, doubling teacher preparation for high and low groups; on the other hand, too many levels can limit the student's development, communication, and peer learning experience of a heterogeneous group. The proper placement of learners involves the administrator's ability to accurately assess the proficiency of students and locate them at the educational level where they can grow to become self-determined learners of the academic communities into which they seek entry.

Placing students with varying degrees of proficiency at optimal levels of instruction is a powerful determinant of their motivation and learning. Except for absolute zero-proficiency students, placement is usually done through standardized or local tests, in some cases a battery of such tests. This type of placement of international students in an intensive multilevel program is more an art than a science. There are no standardized tests or locally devised measures of global language proficiency that assess completely a learner's language competence. The fact that the question—what is second/foreign language acquisition?—is only partially answered after many years of productive research results should suggest to us a more circumspect approach that balances accuracy with fairness and judgment.

The newcomer to the administration of placement is well-advised to rely on multiple measures: know the history of a student's tests, prior language educational experience, self-assessment, and student's evaluation of his test performance, if possible. In placing students, administrators need to be careful not to reify the concepts used, that is, for example, create beginners because we define them as such.

Testing

Placement judgments based on an application of the testing instrument alone, the use of a single test, need not be final. Tests can be retaken under more optimal conditions, or alternative tests used (due to problems with acclimatization, poor lighting, excessive noise, balky computers, poor audio recordings, etc.). Accommodations such as extra time, administering in small groups, pretest support and instruction, and in-test tools (e.g., dictionaries) are now being considered in the testing of ELLs (see Kopriva, 2008) in order to arrive at judgments that reduce measurement error and improve test fairness.

Student placements may be assessed by having teachers provide feedback after the student has spent a few days in class. Indeed, students themselves should also be consulted on whether their placed level is working out or not. Consensus and agreement are important in deciding a placement that is satisfactory to everyone vested in the decision—students, teachers, and administrators. Policies explicitly stating how placement occurs and the processes and procedures for appealing placement decisions are important to communicate with students as well as teachers and staff. Instruction is improved when students believe they are learning at the right level, and a public, democratic process of arriving at decisions builds trust in community.

Directed Self-Placement

Placement is a traditional concern in multilevel IEPs. As with curriculum, innovation in testing may be successfully explored and introduced by a teacher-become-administrator through experimentation with a selection of students to be placed. In addition to the accommodation approach suggested above, another approach is self-assessment. This new approach is perhaps farthest from the traditional approach at IEPs, but is consistent with movements in the assessment of composition in university settings.

Directed self-placement (DSP), also called learner-directed assessment, is suitable for adult learners and one of the most effective ways to develop critical self-awareness, and thus learning, through testing. In addition, the empowering characteristic of self-assessment blends well with the objectives of a student-centered curriculum. Finally, it has the administrative advantages of being quick, cost-efficient, and democratic.

While not yet a substitute for all placement testing, it certainly has a place in placement procedures at IEPs, especially on an experimental basis requiring administrative leadership (see Ekbatani & Pierson, 2000).

In DSP, students decide which IEP courses to take, perhaps within groups of predetermined courses. Students can be given the choice whether to take a traditional test or to volunteer for DSP placement, as there is evidence that some cultures may underestimate and others overestimate the students' ability. DSP can be done either prior to attendance or on site. The advantage of doing it prior to attendance is that the results can be compared with other records (e.g., previous test scores, grades, teacher reports). It may even be implemented online. To effectively use DSP in an IEP environment, an instrument needs to be constructed and piloted with both teachers and students. The instrument must contain the criteria the IEP feels is valid for placement at the levels concerned. In addition to background information, the instrument could employ simplified versions of a common framework, such as the Council of Europe scheme. Here is a sample of the entry level (called "Breakthrough") descriptor in the form of a checklist:

Instruction: Check all of the following you can do.

____ 1. Can understand familiar everyday expressions.

____ 2. Can use familiar everyday expressions.

____ 3. Can use very basic phrases to meet needs to eat, travel, and rent an apartment or room.

____ 4. Can introduce yourself.

____ 5. Can introduce others.

____ 6. Can ask or answer questions about where you live, people you know, and things you own.

Descriptor checklists can be formulated for each IEP level, and a placement decision made based on the percentage of items checked off. Of course, the overall length of the questionnaire checklist should be limited to the length of the traditional placement test in order to avoid fatigue when administered on site.

Another version of a self-assessment instrument focuses on skills. Here is an example about listening in English (from Strong-Krause in Ekbatani & Pierson, 2000):

English Language Teachers as Program Administrators

Instruction: Circle the letter of the description that best matches how difficult it is for you to **understand** spoken English.

A. It is very hard. I can understand a few words or phrases in English, but I don't understand most of what I hear. I like people to talk slowly.

B. It is hard. I can understand some parts of what I hear. I can understand if I know the topic. Many times I need what I hear repeated.

C. It is quite easy. I generally understand most of what I hear. There are some words I don't know.

D. It is easy. I can understand basically everything I hear in English.

Both the descriptor and the skills/task versions can be adapted to the number of levels provided by the IEP. The skills/task version lends itself to selective direct sampling (e.g., using actual recorded passage with questions). It also lends itself to providing a concrete task description prior to the difficulty scale, such as the following writing task (Strong-Krause, 2000, p. 268):

You read a 3-page magazine article in your native language about a strange insect that lives in a certain jungle around the world. Now you must write a summary in English of the article. You tell about where and how the insect lives and describe its life cycle. The main objective of this assignment is to write a summary so clear that someone reading your summary would understand the main points without having to read the original article.

Alternative methods of assessment hold much promise for determining placement and promotion in IEP environments. Teachers-becoming-administrators are well positioned to innovate and thus combine their interest in teaching and research with administration.

REFLECTIVE BREAK

- How might directed self-placement work in your teaching environment?

5

Conclusion

Administering an intensive English program is a many-splendoured thing, to paraphrase Robert Kaplan, a well-known administrator. Teachers who wish to prepare for any number of roles in administering an English language program can combine their formal education with subsequent self-development.

This short book has presented only a few issues in administering programs: managing personnel, student recruitment, selecting instructors, balancing continuity and innovation in curriculum and technology, and evaluation, particularly in terms of student placement. Each offers a basic view of the administrative functions while remaining sensitive to the associated complexities.

Teachers who wish to become administrators are advised to follow up this introduction with further self-study, in particular the references cited throughout. Informed teachers can add substantially to the administrative core of many language programs, and through continued self-development can give shape to these important aspects of learning and cultural interaction.

References

American Council of Teachers of Foreign Languages. (ACTFL). (2012). *ACTFL proficiency guidelines 2012.*Retrieved from http://www.actfl.org /files/public/ACTFLProficiencyGuidelines2012_FINAL.pdf

Atkinson, D., & Ramanathan, V. (1995). Cultures of writing: An ethnographic comparison of L1 and L2 university writing/language programs. *TESOL Quarterly, 29,* 539–568.

Brown, H. D. (1995). *The elements of language curriculum: A systematic approach to program development.* Boston, MA: Heinle & Heinle.

Brown, H. D. (2004). *Language assessment: Principles and classroom practices.* White Plains, NY: Longman/Pearson Education.

Christison, M. A., & Murray, D. (Eds.). (2009). *Leadership in English language education: Theoretical foundations and practical skills for changing times.* Mahwah, NJ: Erlbaum.

Christison, M. A., & Stoller, F. L. (Eds.). (1997). *A handbook for language program administrators* (1st ed.). Miami, FL: Alta Books.

Christison, M. A., & Stoller, F. L. (2012). *A handbook for language program administrators* (2nd ed.). Burlingame, CA: Alta Books.

Cohen, A. (1994). *Assessing language ability in the classroom* (2nd ed.). Boston, MA: Heinle & Heinle.

Council of Europe. (1996). *A common European framework for language learning and teaching: Draft of a framework proposal.* Strasbourg, France: Council of Europe.

Dimmitt, N., & Dantas-Whitney, M. (Eds.). (2002). *Intensive English programs in postsecondary settings.* Alexandria, VA: TESOL.

Ekbatani, G., & Pierson, H. (2000). *Learner-directed assessment in ESL.* Mahwah, NJ: Erlbaum.

Farrell, T. S. C. (2007). *Reflective language teaching: From research to practice.* New York, NY: Continuum.

Gebhard, J. G. (2010). *What do international students think and feel: Adapting to U.S. college life and culture.* Ann Arbor, MI: University of Michigan Press.

Heaney, L. (2009). *Guide to international student recruitment* (2nd ed.). Washington, DC: NAFSA.

Huot, B., & Schendel, E. (2002). A working methodology of assessment for writing program administrators. In I. Ward & W. J. Carpenter (Eds.), *The Allyn & Bacon sourcebook for writing program administrators* (pp. 207–227). New York, NY: Longman.

Institute of International Education (IIE). (2011). *Open doors 2011: Report on international educational exchange.* Retrieved from http://www.iie.org /Research-and-Publications/Open-Doors

International Society for Technology in Education (ISTE). (2012). *National Educational Technology Standards for Teachers (NETS.T).* Retrieved from http://www.iste.org/docs/pdfs/nets-t-standards.pdf?sfvrsn=2

Kopriva, R. J. (2008). *Improving testing for English language learners.* New York, NY: Routledge.

Kram, K. E. (1983). Phases of the mentor relationship. *Academy of Management Journal, 26*(4), 608–625.

MacDonald, L. (2010*).* The "virtual language lab" virtually painless, simply real. *International Association of Language Learning Technology Journal, 41*(1). Retrieved from http://www.iallt.org/iallt_journal/the_virtual_language _lab_virtually_painless_simply_real

Markee, N. (1997). *Managing curricular innovation.* Cambridge, England: Cambridge University Press.

Pennington, M. C. (Ed.). (1991). *Building better English language programs.* Washington, DC: NAFSA.

Richards, J. C., & Farrell, T .S. C. (2005). *Professional development for language teachers: Strategies for teacher learning.* Cambridge, England: Cambridge University Press.

Roby, W. B. (2004). Technology in the service of foreign language learning: The case of the language laboratory. *Handbook of research on educational communications and technology* (2nd ed., pp. 523–541). Mahwah, NJ: Erlbaum.

Saville-Troike, M. (2006). *Introducing second language acquisition*. Cambridge, England: Cambridge University Press.

Stoller, F. L. (1992). Taxonomy of intensive English program innovations. *Journal of Intensive English Studies, 6,* 1–25.

Strong-Krause, D. (2000). Exploring the effectiveness of self-assessment strategies in ESL placement. In G. Ekbatani and H. Pierson (Eds.), *Learner-directed assessment in ESL* (pp. 255–278.). New York, NY: Taylor & Frances Routledge.

TESOL. (2003). *TESOL/NCATE program standards: Standards for the accreditation of initial programs in P-12 ESL teacher education.* Retrieved from http://www.ncate.org/ProgramStandards/TESOL/TesolStd.pdf

TESOL. (2011). *TESOL technology standards: Description, implementation, integration.* Alexandria, VA.

TESOL. (2012). *Preparing effective teachers of English language learners: Practical applications for the TESOL P–12 professional teaching standards.* Alexandria, VA.

Whitbeck, M., & Healey, D. (1997). Technology and the language program administrator. In M. A. Christison & F. Stoller (Eds.), *Handbook for language program administrators* (pp. 253–273). Burlingame, CA: Alta Book Center.

White, R., Hockley, A., van der Horst Jansen, J., & Laughner, M. S. (2008). *From teacher to manager: Managing language teaching organizations.* Cambridge, England: Cambridge University Press.

Also Available in the English Language Teacher Development Series

www.tesol.org/bookstore
tesolpubs@brightkey.net
Request a copy for review
Request a Distributor Policy